CW00972451

To witness is to let
simply by virtue of
witnesses simply b
have been brought into his light, now he appoints us
to bring his light to others. This is what witness is.

Over the next six and a half weeks these Lent
reflections take you on a journey through the Gospel
of John and give you an opportunity to explore what
the gift of Jesus and the challenge of Jesus mean for
you, in the context of your daily life.

In the middle of John's Gospel is a verse that goes to
the heart of it:

*Jesus said, 'I came that they might have life, and have it
abundantly'*

It is our prayer that this booklet helps and
encourages you as you take hold of God's gift of life
and live it – to the full. God offers us this life for the
sake of others. The light he gives us in Jesus Christ is
not to be hidden but to shine – it's a gift to be lived
and shared. Indeed, the more we share it and let it
shine, the brighter it burns.

Archbishop Justin Welby

Archbishop John Sentamu

HOW TO USE THIS BOOK

#LiveLent – Let Your Light Shine will help you ask yourself two questions:

- How can I receive God's life more fully?
- How can I live God's life more generously, imaginatively and joyfully, in such a way that others can see it, hear it and take hold of it themselves?

Each day there is a short **reading** from the Gospel of John, followed by a brief reflection. This is followed by an invitation to simply stop for a moment and to **pause** and reflect on what the passage might mean to us.

Having paused, it follows naturally that we go on to **pray** about our own discipleship and to ask that others too may discover the fullness of God's life, as we pray in the words Jesus gave us... *Thy kingdom come.*

Finally, there is an invitation to **witness**, to do something each day to help make God's life a reality for others, through your words and your life... *Thy will be done.*

Week 1
GIFT

The light shines in the darkness, and the darkness did not overcome it.

JOHN 1.5

All that we are, and all that we see and know of the world around us, is gift from God. The breath that brings our bodies to life – and the beauty that causes us to catch that same breath.

Yet life is fragile, often painful and sometimes dark. God speaks again into the darkness. God gives again. God makes himself known, fully, in Jesus Christ, the light that shines in the darkness.

The light that shines in the darkness and is not overcome is not earned or bought. It is not the private possession of a few. It is a gift for all. It is Jesus – God's gift to any who welcome and receive him.

This week, thank God for the gift of life, and for the gift that is Jesus. And try to be a gift to others by letting some of God's light shine through you.

Ash Wednesday, Week 1

Life

READ John 1.1-5

'What has come into being in him was life, and the life was the light of all people.'

Today is Ash Wednesday, a day to remember that we are 'dust and ashes' and to look our mortality in the face. We do so not to make us miserable or morbid. The reason is actually just the opposite. As we embrace our mortality we find freedom to take hold afresh of the gift of life.

Like Lent, the Gospel of John begins with words about life. The beautiful diverse and fragile life of creation. The personal, precious and complex life of our own existence. All this is a gift, spoken into being by God through Jesus, the Word.

The life we live is not always beautiful or easy. It is often dark. As we see within it the gift of God and the beauty of God, we discern a light that shines brightly and can never be put out.

PAUSE

Take time today to see the signs of life around you and within you; and say thank you.

PRAY ...*Thy kingdom come*

In a moment of stillness, acknowledge God as the source of all life and, as you are able, place your own mortal life in God's eternal hands.

WITNESS ...*Thy will be done*

Amid the fragility of life around you, offer a word of gentleness and strength. Amid the darkness of life, be a presence that brings light and hope.

Thursday, Week 1

Love

READ John 1.6-13

To all who received him, who believed in his name, he gave power to become children of God.

Jesus, the Word through whom all creation exists, becomes part of that creation, born as a baby in vulnerability. He embraces and knows all the fragility, beauty and sorrow of life.

As we look at Jesus we see how life can be when it is lived to the full – a life marked by trust and forgiveness, by prayer and faith, by goodness and grace even when things are tough.

As we receive Jesus we receive the gift of his life. Our lives, like his, shaped in every moment and each situation by relationship with God the Father. It is love which gives us life: the deep unconditional love of God who calls us his children.

PAUSE

Take time today to think about what it means for you to receive Jesus and the life and love God offers us through him.

PRAY ...*Thy kingdom come*

Ask God for the gift of faith to open your heart to the love of God that is always open to you; and pray for all the children of God.

WITNESS ...*Thy will be done*

Make time today to live the unconditional gift of God's love. In a relationship, seek simply to give, to love and not seek anything in return.

Friday, Week 1
Glory

READ John 1.14-18

No one has ever seen God. It is God the only Son, who is close to the Father's heart, who has made him known.

John's claim in this verse is both bold and simple. Jesus makes visible the invisible God. 'We have seen his glory,' John says. The Word, which brought creation into being, is fully present and known in a human life. It is, as John puts it, 'made flesh'. God embodied. God incarnate. God with us.

If you stop and think about it, this says something pretty amazing about God – that he can be known and seen in this way – and it says something equally amazing about a human life – that God can be seen in us, whoever we are.

And just note what qualifies Jesus to do this. He is, John says, the one who is close to the Father's heart. Isn't that wonderful?

PAUSE

How does Jesus make God visible to you? What do his life and words tell you about who God is and what God is like?

PRAY ...*Thy kingdom come*

Glory is seeing something of God in the ordinariness of our humanity. Pray that others may see God's glory in you and thank him for those who reveal God's glory to you.

WITNESS ...*Thy will be done*

In what ordinary situation might you bring a bit of God's surprising glory? It might begin, as it did for Jesus, by taking time to be close to God's heart.

Saturday, Week 1

See

READ John 1.35-42

John the Baptist saw Jesus coming towards him and declared, 'Here is the Lamb of God who takes away the sin of the world.'

The short first week of this Lent journey through John's Gospel concludes with words of John the Baptist. He points to Jesus, as the one through whom there is forgiveness and peace with God, and says, Look, See, Receive.

That is, in a nutshell, the invitation of John's Gospel. Look at Jesus. See God in him. Receive Life through him. It's an invitation that comes to us from Jesus himself. When two of John the Baptist's followers approached him, he didn't give them a long essay or a list of rules, he simply said: 'Come and see.'

That's where our discipleship begins and ends, and it's also the heart of our witness and evangelism. Come and look, and as you see, receive.

PAUSE

Take time at the end of this week, to reflect on the gift that Jesus Christ brings to your life. What words characterise, for you, that gift?

PRAY ...*Thy kingdom come*

Thank God for Jesus Christ and all that is yours through him. Pray for those you know to whom God is saying: come, see, receive.

WITNESS ...*Thy will be done*

Today, try to be a visible sign of a life that is both forgiven and forgiving. It might simply be a word, or a handshake, or picking up the phone.

Week 2
CHANGE

Jesus did this, the first of his signs, in Cana of Galilee, and revealed his glory; and his disciples believed in him.

JOHN 2.11

The Gospel of John describes the miracles of Jesus as signs. Jesus brings healing and transformation, curing the sick, feeding the hungry, raising the dead and changing 700 litres of water into the very best wine.

These signs help us see and understand the change that Jesus brings to our lives and our communities. The life and person of Jesus tell us that God is with us in the joys and in the mess of life. They also tell us that God's presence with us is not passive; it brings transformation. John calls it God's glory. God with us, active and life-changing.

This week is an opportunity to reflect on God's glorious transformation and to pray that we might be more open to all that God wants to do in our lives and our situations.

First Sunday of Lent, Week 2

Make New

READ John 2.1-11

'The steward tasted the water that had become wine, and did not know where it came from.'

Jesus attends a wedding at Cana at which disaster strikes: the wine runs out! Jesus' mother asks for his help. At Jesus' instructions water is poured into some large jars, they are filled to the brim. As the water is then drawn out from the jars it is transformed. Water has become wine. Not just any wine, but the best.

John describes this miracle as 'the first of his signs'. The glory of God, seen in the Word made flesh, is seen also in this miracle of transformation. God takes the ordinary and the exhausted and makes it new.

That's the glory of God. It's seen in Jesus, and it's all around us.

PAUSE

Are there areas of your life which have 'run out' or become weary? Name them, own them and offer them like an empty water jar to God.

PRAY ...*Thy kingdom come*

Ask God to show you the unexpected life and beauty that, through his transforming presence, can be found within you and in others.

WITNESS ...*Thy will be done*

In wisdom, love and gentleness, seek to draw out something new and life-giving from a person or situation you encounter.

Monday, Week 2

Make Room

READ John 2.12-16

He drove all of them out of the temple, poured out the coins of the money-changers and overturned their tables.

Jesus travels to Jerusalem and visits the temple. Where there should have been space for prayer he found a crowded marketplace.

The outer area of the temple should have been set apart as a place of prayer for strangers, or Gentiles, and others who were not permitted to go into the inner areas.

Jesus was angry that people on the edge of society were pushed to the edges of the temple, too – prevented from finding, in his Father's house, a place to pray and meet God. He takes things into his own hands with determination!

PAUSE

In what ways can you make space for others to encounter God today? Do you possibly need to do the same for yourself?

PRAY ...*Thy kingdom come*

Pray for all who find themselves pushed away when they seek to find God, especially for anyone on your heart today. Pray for the Church, that God would turn us inside out.

WITNESS ...*Thy will be done*

Make time today to create some space for somebody else. Pause long enough to notice when someone is pushed out or pushed away and do something about it.

Tuesday, Week 2

Start Again

READ John 3.1-10

*'The wind blows where it chooses, you do
not know where it comes from. So it is with
everyone who is born of the Spirit.'*

Nicodemus comes to see Jesus in the
privacy of the night. He's respectable and
religious. Jesus seems to prize neither.
Nicodemus seeks him out because Jesus
has a grasp of life and truth that, despite
Nicodemus' education and his religious
expertise, has eluded him.

Jesus tells him he needs to start again, to be born again. It's how Jesus describes what happens when we make a new start with God.

Let God's Spirit, as unpredictable as the wind, bring life to you. Don't force it. Let it happen. That's his message to Nicodemus, and to us.

PAUSE

In what ways is God's interaction with your life like the wind? When has it felt like a breeze, and when like a gale?

PRAY ...*Thy kingdom come*

Ask God for the strength to let go of pride, fear, worry, anger or other burdens and pray: 'Breathe on me breath of God, fill me with life anew.'

WITNESS ...*Thy will be done*

Where might the wind of God's Spirit blow you today? Be a breath of fresh air for someone and help them make a new start.

Wednesday, Week 2

Set Free

READ John 3.14-21

'God did not send the Son into the world to condemn the world, but in order that the world might be saved through him.'

Jesus continues his conversation with Nicodemus. He leads him to see that what lies at the heart of the life he is talking about is love.

The life of God that Jesus makes visible is love. The new life that the wind of the Spirit breathes into us, is love. The reason that Jesus is in the world is love.

God's love doesn't condemn or exclude. God's love is always giving, always reaching out and always seeking to bring life to all it touches. It's a love which sets us free. It's a love seen most deeply and most clearly in Jesus' life, in his death and in his resurrection.

PAUSE

Why is that we find it all too easy to replace love with condemnation? We can even do it in how we talk about God.

PRAY ...*Thy kingdom come*

Ask God to help you know how much you are loved. Ask God to help you love others with that same unconditional acceptance.

WITNESS ...*Thy will be done*

Offer a word today that encourages and welcomes. Resist the temptation to jump to judge or condemn. It might help to start by listening.

Thursday, Week 2

Thirst

READ John 4.1-15

'Sir, give me this water, so that I may never be thirsty or have to keep coming here to draw water.'

Jesus travels in the heat of the day and sits down to rest at a well in Samaria. He is on his own and without any means of drawing water from the well. He is thirsty.

He asks a woman for a drink. She has perhaps chosen deliberately to avoid meeting others by coming to the well when other villagers would be resting. His request breaks through social and religious barriers and initiates a conversation.

Jesus, sensing her own inner thirst, offers her the water that can refresh a lonely longing heart. The water of God's love.

PAUSE

Where is there a sense of thirst in your life? What is the source of that thirst? How do you seek to satisfy it?

PRAY ...*Thy kingdom come*

Ask God's grace to drink deeply of the water of God's love. Pray for all who are thirsty today. Pray for those who long for love and thirst for God.

WITNESS ...*Thy will be done*

Make time today to give a gift which brings refreshment. Buy someone a drink. Stop and listen. Be open to starting a conversation about the love of God.

Friday, Week 2

Believe

READ John 4.46-54

Jesus said to him, 'Go; your son will live.' The man believed the word that Jesus spoke to him and started on his way.'

Back in Cana, a government official begs Jesus to come over to Capernaum and heal his dying son. It's a desperate heartfelt plea.

Jesus declines to go with him to his house, but instead simply tells him to go home, promising him that his son will live. The official believes. For him faith means returning home, leaving Jesus but finding his son alive. It didn't happen in the way he thought, but it happened.

John tells us this was the second sign that Jesus gave us. It's a great story of faith in God and a joyful sign of the life and transformation that faith unlocks.

PAUSE

Take time today ... for faith. What's going on in your life at the moment that calls for trust? What steps does your faith in God invite you to take?

PRAY *...Thy kingdom come*

Pray for a courageous, generous and gentle faith. Pray, too, for all those who seek healing for those they love.

WITNESS *...Thy will be done*

Step out in faith today. Take a risk for God and someone else. Build a bridge. Ask for help. Offer to pray. Speak gently about your faith.

Saturday, Week 2

Stand Up

READ John 5.1-11

Jesus said to him, 'Stand up, take your mat and walk.' At once the man was made well, and he took up his mat and began to walk.

Jesus returns to Jerusalem. In the city is a pool surrounded by many sick people waiting for the water to be stirred (perhaps by a natural spring). They wait because they believe that at the moment the water is disturbed those who first enter it are healed. For some it is a long and heart-breaking wait.

Jesus sees a man who has always found himself
at the back of the queue. Too ill ever to get to the
water soon enough. He has been ill for 38 years.
Jesus sees him. Jesus speaks to him. Jesus
challenges him. 'Stand up,' he says. The man gets
up and he is healed.

PAUSE
Think back on all that you have learned this week.
Is there one thing you can do to help God bring
change to your life? Do it today. How might you
help bring God's change to others?

PRAY ...*Thy kingdom come*
Pray for all those who today are waiting for help or
healing. Pray for someone who particularly comes to
mind, and ask God to show what you can do to help.

WITNESS ...*Thy will be done*
Don't be frustrated that others seem to find things
easier, stand up and live your faith today as you are,
the person God has made and loves.

Week 3
BREAD

Jesus said to them, 'I am the bread of life. Whoever comes to me will never be hungry, and whoever believes in me will never be thirsty.' JOHN 6.35

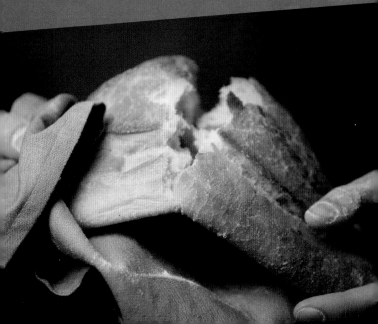

Alongside the seven signs in John's Gospel are seven sayings of Jesus which begin with the words 'I am'. These are not the self-important overblown claims of a superhero but gentle generous invitations to see Jesus and to understand how he shapes our discipleship and friendship with him.

Jesus, the Bread of Life, is the one who makes known truth that is deep and lasting. His life and his words feed those hungry to see how to truly live and love.

He invites us to come to him and be fed, to be nourished and refreshed. He calls us to be those who feed and nurture the lives of others.

Even if we feel the resources and gifts we have are only crumbs, they can, in his hands, become the means of bringing life to others.

Second Sunday of Lent, Week 3

Crumbs

READ John 6.1-9

'There is a boy here who has five barley loaves and two fish. But what are they among so many people?'

The crowds follow Jesus to the far side of lake Galilee, longing to see more, to hear more and, perhaps, to understand more.

It is a deserted place and the people are some distance from their homes. They are hungry. Jesus asks his disciples to find food for them.

Andrew finds a boy with a picnic that he is willing to share. It's one picnic, one boy, and one disciple who found him. It's just crumbs amongst such a crowd of people. But in Jesus' hands it becomes so much more...

PAUSE

What are the 'crumbs' in your life that seem inadequate for you and for those who come to you for help? Faith, love, hope? Time, energy, patience?

PRAY ...*Thy kingdom come*

What might happen if you, like the boy and his picnic, put those 'crumbs' into God's hands? Do it now as you pray, *'Thy kingdom come'*.

WITNESS ...*Thy will be done*

Make time today to feed another with food, love or kindness. Offer what you have, even if it feels inadequate, with thanks and generosity.

Monday, Week 3

Shared

READ John 6.10-14

Then Jesus took the loaves, and when he had given thanks, he distributed them to those who were seated; so also the fish, as much as they wanted.

Jesus receives the loaves, he offers them to God in thanks and blessing, he breaks the bread, and shares it. Picture him doing it. See the pattern of his actions in your imagination.

Receiving, giving thanks, breaking and sharing. It's the familiar pattern in Holy Communion (also called The Eucharist, and The Lord's Supper). It's a pattern for us, for our lives, for our gifts, for all we are and all we receive. It's a pattern to practise – receive, give thanks, hold with open hands before God and share.

The crowd was fed and satisfied. More crumbs were left over and gathered together. It was a miracle. It's another sign of glory. It's the way things work with God. Try it.

PAUSE
Thank God today for the gifts he has placed in your hands. Life, health, people, love, opportunities, abilities... hold them lightly.

PRAY ...*Thy kingdom come*
Pause to pray as Jesus did, receive these gifts, thank God for them and offer them to him and seek his grace and guidance in sharing them.

WITNESS ...*Thy will be done*
Give something away that you've been holding onto. Would it be of more benefit to a foodbank, charity shop, or friend or neighbour?

Tuesday, Week 3

Fear

READ John 6.15-21

'It was now dark, and Jesus had not yet come to them. The lake became rough because a strong wind was blowing.'

After the miracle comes the storm, and Jesus is not there. It often seems to be like that. Moments of wonder and clarity, followed closely by times of confusion and questions.

Jesus has withdrawn into the hills. The disciples are going home across the lake. A storm blows up. They are alone. It is dark.

Jesus does appear, but it's unexpected and unfamiliar. Their response is uncertain and fearful – they think he's a ghost.

Jesus speaks to them: 'It is I, do not be afraid.'

PAUSE

Reflect on those moments—or even seasons—in your life when God seems absent. In what ways has his presence been made known to you again?

PRAY ...*Thy kingdom come*

Pray for those who hunger for God and cannot find him. Pray for those who live today in fear, especially for those known to you.

WITNESS ...*Thy will be done*

How might you, today, bring calm to a storm? Where might an action say 'do not be afraid'?

Wednesday, Week 3

Lasting

READ John 6.22-34

'Do not work for the food that perishes, but for the food that endures for eternal life, which the Son of Man will give you.'

Jesus talks with the crowds about their experience on the far side of the lake and the miracle with the loaves and fishes that fed them. He reminds them of the miraculous manna which appeared each morning and fed people in the desert centuries ago: by the end of the day it was gone.

It's not all about miracles, he says. What matters is what lasts and goes on feeding you. It's easy to look for miracles in our own situations, or for quick answers or simple solutions.

Jesus offers something different: bread that lasts, truth that feeds, love that lives, life eternal.

PAUSE

What in your life has short-lived worth? What has lasting value? In which do you invest most time?

PRAY ...*Thy kingdom come*

Pray for all who are seeking something in their lives that lasts. Pray for those you know and love, that they might find Christ to be the bread that endures.

WITNESS ...*Thy will be done*

In a world where so much is transient, make time to do something for someone else with a lasting consequence.

Thursday, Week 3

I am the Bread of Life

READ John 6.35-40

'I am the bread of life. Whoever comes to me will never be hungry, and whoever believes in me will never be thirsty.'

The crowd asks Jesus for bread that doesn't go stale, for food that will feed the world with a life that lasts. 'Sir, give us this bread always.'

It's a cry we hear from different voices and in different places across the world today. Hunger is real. It's physical, emotional, social and spiritual.

Jesus' answer is simply to point to himself. Come to me. Come and see. Look, see, receive.

This, my life, lived and shared, is bread for the world. Listen to my words, see my signs, know my love, receive my life as your food and drink. I am the bread of life.

PAUSE

What does it mean to you for Jesus to be the 'bread of life'? In what ways does he offer you something that lasts and satisfies?

PRAY ...*Thy kingdom come*

Pray for all who are hungry today. Pray for those you know who are looking for something to feed their bodies or their souls.

WITNESS ...*Thy will be done*

Look for an opportunity to invite someone to consider how the words, life and daily presence of Jesus might be bread of life for them.

Friday, Week 3

Reality

READ John 6.66-69

Simon Peter answered him, 'Lord, to whom can we go? You have the words of eternal life.'

Jesus challenges the crowd who are looking for more miracles and he confronts the religious for resting on their ancestral laurels. People begin to walk away.

Even some of his followers seem to be puzzled and disenchanted. This teaching is too difficult for us, they say.

Jesus offers life but it seems not everybody's ready or able to take hold of it.

His twelve close disciples remain. Peter puts it bluntly. You're the real thing. We've seen it. We've heard it. We've met you. How can we go anywhere else?

PAUSE

Reflect on the words of Jesus that are 'the real thing' to you. What is it about Jesus that makes you want to follow him even when it is hard or puzzling?

PRAY ...*Thy kingdom come*

Pray for those you know who struggle to follow Christ. Pray that they might see the reality of Christ even in the mess and muddle.

WITNESS ...*Thy will be done*

Make time today to live the reality of something Jesus said, to be a signpost to someone who is struggling to see the way to go.

Saturday, Week 3

Drink

READ John 7.37-39

On the last day of the festival, the great day, while Jesus was standing there, he cried out, 'Let anyone who is thirsty come to me, and let the one who believes in me drink.'

Jesus returns to Jerusalem for a religious festival. It is a risky visit, because already some people are looking for a way to kill him. His teaching has puzzled some and provoked others.

However, some people, intrigued by his teaching, want to know more. Jesus explains to them that all he says and does flows from his relationship with God; a life-giving union of love and trust.

Again he offers his invitation. Come to me. Come, see, listen and receive. If you are thirsty, he says, come to me and drink. Receive the Spirit who, like a river of living water, is the one who draws us and all the world into relationship with God. As it was for Jesus so it can be for us.

PAUSE

Think back on all that you have learned this week. Is there one thing you can do to know more of the reality that Jesus the bread and water of life brings?

PRAY ...*Thy kingdom come*

Pray for all who are thirsty for water or for life. Pray for all who long for God and are puzzled or confounded.

WITNESS ...*Thy will be done*

Make some time to write down the story of your relationship with God, how it began, how it has grown, what it means today. Look for an opportunity to share the story.

Week 4
LIGHT

Jesus spoke to them, saying,
'I am the light of the world.
Whoever follows me will never
walk in darkness but will have
the light of life.' **JOHN 8.12**

John tells us that Jesus came into the world as a light in the darkness. That light, he says, is the life that is in all people. Yet it was a light that was recognised and welcomed by only a few.

Jesus the light reveals the blindness in the hearts and lives of those he met. It is seen most vividly in his confrontation with those who brought a woman to him, wanting to test him — and to stone her.

Jesus the light, through the gift of forgiveness and healing, brings freedom. Jesus the light brings the liberation of seeing ourselves, and others, as we truly are. More than anything, the light of Jesus helps us see as God sees, with love and compassion and with hope.

This week is an opportunity to reflect on the light that Jesus brings to your life and your situation.

Third Sunday of Lent, Week 4

Anger

READ John 8.1-6

The scribes and the Pharisees brought a woman who had been caught in adultery; and made her stand before all of them.

Early one morning in Jerusalem Jesus visits the temple. People listen to his words. Some hear a voice speaking with love, truth, wisdom and insight.

Others seem unable to listen to the words, but only to see one who had no right to speak in that place, or their place. They become angry.

They bring a woman, a 'sinner', to Jesus. We'll show her. We'll show him.

Jesus sees a gang of men with fists, stones, anger and blindness seeking to silence his words with violence.

PAUSE

When were you last angry? What caused it? What was its effect on you and others?

PRAY ...*Thy kingdom come*

Pray that your anger might be less about defending yourself and more a motivation to seek the good and well-being of others.

WITNESS ...*Thy will be done*

Make a conscious effort today to unclench a fist, put down a stone, and reach out an open hand of forgiveness and love.

Monday, Week 4

Look

READ John 8.7-9

When they kept on questioning him, he straightened up and said to them, 'Let anyone among you who is without sin be the first to throw a stone at her.'

Jesus writes on the ground. He pauses. Maybe he's drawing a line in the sand.

The men stop too, waiting. Maybe they are beginning to listen to their own hearts, maybe they are beginning to open their eyes to the woman.

Look at yourselves, Jesus says. Start there and then you might be able to see others more truly. Look at yourself first and if you still feel you have the right to throw a stone, then do it.

Anger dissipates in shame and in a recovering of sight. They walk away, beginning with the eldest.

PAUSE

When we are in pain, or helpless, or under attack; it's easy to blame others. What helps you stop, listen and begin to see a situation and yourself more clearly?

PRAY ...*Thy kingdom come*

Let Jesus speak to you in quietness, and as you listen, know yourself as you are; know that, as you are, you are loved.

WITNESS ...*Thy will be done*

Stop. Listen. Take a fresh look. Do something to change a situation or relationship. Speak a word of gentle truth.

Tuesday, Week 4

Compassion

READ John 8.10-11

Jesus said, 'Neither do I condemn you. Go your way, and from now on do not sin again.'

Jesus waits. The violent and the voyeurs wander slowly away. The tension eases, a sense of calm gradually returns.

The woman stays near Jesus. Vulnerable and unsure. Is she now at this stranger's mercy?

Where have they gone, your judges? asks Jesus. Is no one left?

Jesus does not walk away.

He stays and sees. He waits and loves. He does not condemn.

It's called compassion.

PAUSE
Where is God asking you not to walk away, but to stay and see, and love with deep compassion?

PRAY ...*Thy kingdom come*
Pray today for eyes to see those around you not as objects to be judged or stereotypes to be labelled but people who are loved.

WITNESS ...*Thy will be done*
Make time today to sit with someone, waiting, listening, loving; and speak, when you do, with compassion.

Wednesday, Week 4

I am the light of the world

READ John 8.12-15

Jesus spoke to them, saying, 'I am the light of the world. Whoever follows me will never walk in darkness but will have the light of life.'

This is the second of Jesus stunning self-descriptions, the 'I am' sayings: I am the light of the world.

Massive claims, but not overblown self-importance. Rather these seven sayings are Jesus' invitation to see him, to come to him and to find life in him.

Come, see, receive.

As we come to Jesus. As we spend time with him, listening to his words and walking his way. So we begin to see more clearly, for he is light.

In that light, we see ourselves, we see others and we see the world differently. In that light we know ourselves and we know him, and we find the darkness is banished.

PAUSE

How might the light of Christ shine more brightly in and through your life? What can you do today to enable that to happen?

PRAY ...*Thy kingdom come*

Most merciful redeemer, friend and brother, may we know you more clearly, love you more dearly, and follow you more nearly, day by day. Amen.

WITNESS ...*Thy will be done*

Make time today for light. Speak truth. Pray with faith. Love deeply. Banish darkness.

Thursday, Week 4

Truth

READ John 8.31-33

Jesus said, 'You will know the truth, and the truth will make you free.'

Like light in the darkness, truth reveals what is there. Truth shows us ourselves as well as the world around us.

Truth can hurt. It can take to time to hear it.

Truth can challenge. We might need to revisit some of the things we have believed.

But the real test of truth is that, as Jesus says, it sets us free. Truth never ties us up in knots or beats us down. Never.

PAUSE
What are the ways in which Jesus brings truth to you – to your mind, your heart and to your life?

PRAY ...*Thy kingdom come*
Pray for those who are beaten down or knotted up. Pray for yourself when it feels like that for you. May the Spirit of truth set us all free, truly free.

WITNESS ...*Thy will be done*
Take an opportunity to share the truth of Jesus in a way that brings freedom and life to others.

Friday, Week 4

Forgiveness

READ John 8.34-38

'So if the Son makes you free, you will be free indeed.'

Whatever words we might use to describe it and however we would understand it, we would probably all agree that sin ties us up.

It is true personally and corporately. It's the effect we see of wrong actions, words, and attitudes whether lies, greed, oppression or fear. Sin damages, destroys and imprisons.

'Everyone who commits sin is a slave to sin,' says Jesus. Our slavery to sin has a massive effect on those around us, on people elsewhere in the world and on the fragile creation in which we live.

The truth and love, the life and death, of Jesus sets us free from the power of sin to tie us up. That freedom comes as we take hold of God's gift of forgiveness.

PAUSE

Take some time today to think about the effect of sin in your life and on those you love or work with. Ask God's forgiveness. Ask for strength to put things right.

PRAY ...*Thy kingdom come*

Pray for all those whose lives are damaged by sin, either their own or others'. Pray that Christ would set them free.

WITNESS ...*Thy will be done*

Give a gift – by offering forgiveness, or by receiving forgiveness. Let that gift unlock your heart as well.

Saturday, Week 4

Sight

READ John 9.1-12

'The man called Jesus made mud, spread it on my eyes, and said to me, "Go to Siloam and wash." Then I went and washed and received my sight.'

This week's reflections have centred on aspects of being set free. Anger, fear and sin giving way to light, truth, love and forgiveness.

For John, the great theme is sight. What makes us spiritually 'blind' and who enables us to see? What pushes us to live in darkness and who brings us into the light?

It is brought together in this story of the man who had been blind from birth, and the ensuing debate between Jesus and the religious leaders.

The blind man, unnoticed and ignored by many, is seen by Jesus. With mud and water, through touch and love, by the power of God, Jesus heals him.

PAUSE

What blind spots are there in your life? What might the light of Christ enable and encourage you to see?

PRAY ...*Thy kingdom come*

Ask God to help you see, more clearly, the beauty and the needs around you, and the goodness and the muddle within you, and God in it all.

WITNESS ...*Thy will be done*

Make time today to see someone, or a tricky situation, in a new way. Let God use that new perspective to help you make a difference.

Week 5
LIFE

Jesus said, 'I came that they may have life, and have it abundantly. I am the good shepherd. The good shepherd lays down his life for the sheep.' **JOHN 10.10-11**

The greatest gift that Jesus offers is life. The life he brings is generous and joyful, liberating and purposeful. It is life lived to the full.

Jesus brings life through his words and his actions. He brings life because, like a good shepherd, he loves deeply and personally and at great cost. He lets go of his life so we can receive life.

The life that Jesus brings is death-defeating. He is the resurrection who weeps with Mary, invites Martha to believe and calls Lazarus out of the tomb.

This week's readings invite you to reflect on how you might bring resurrection and hope where there is grief, despair and death. How might you let your light shine?

**Fourth Sunday of Lent,
Mothering Sunday, Week 5**

I am the gate

READ John 10.1-9

*'I am the gate. Whoever enters by me will be
saved, and will come in and go out and find
pasture.'*

I am, Jesus says, for the third time.
A shepherd guards the entrance to
the sheep fold. My body is the door.
I am the gate.

It's an image of protection; there is safety to be found in Jesus.

It's an image of provision, there is nourishment to be found through Jesus.

It's an image of personal, costly commitment.

Jesus the gate, like the mothers we celebrate today, protects and provides for us with love that is willing to put itself between us and danger.

PAUSE

What or who offers you security? Where does your life find its nourishment? How would you say Jesus meets these needs in you?

PRAY ...*Thy kingdom come*

Pray for all who do not know today the love and protection of a mother or another carer. Pray for those God has given you to guard and provide for.

WITNESS ...*Thy will be done*

Make time today for the most vulnerable people in society: refugees, homeless people, the exploited, the very young, the old. Do something practical.

Monday, Week 5

Abundantly

READ John 10.10

'I came that they may have life, and have it abundantly.'

At the centre of the Gospel of John is this verse that goes to the heart of the Good News of Jesus. Jesus is Good News for the world and for your friends because he came to enable all people to have life, not just some and not just a half-life. Abundant life. For all.

Jesus' most strongly worded conversations were with religious leaders. Too often the effect of their teaching and demands on others was to stifle, restrict and burden.

This angered Jesus because that religious expression misrepresented God whose deepest desire for us, and his great gift to us, is life. Life in all its fullness.

PAUSE
Take time today ... to consider the things that restrict you and prevent you from living life to the full. What is their root and what is their effect?

PRAY ...*Thy kingdom come*
Ask God to help you to be free to live his abundant life. Pray for those you know whose lives are burdened or restricted, or who struggle to receive God's gift of life.

WITNESS ...*Thy will be done*
Make time today for a bit of joyful extravagance! Live life to the full. Perhaps have a party, invite some friends and perhaps even some you don't yet know well.

Tuesday, Week 5

I am the Good Shepherd

READ John 10.11-18

'I am the good shepherd. The good shepherd lays down his life for the sheep.'

I am, Jesus says, for the fourth time. A good shepherd cares for his sheep because he has invested his life in them, unlike the one merely hired to look after them.

He knows his sheep and they know him. His care is personal, based on a relationship of love and trust.

The Good Shepherd will do anything for their protection and well-being, even giving his own life.

It's a poignant, powerful image which begins to point us to Holy Week and the journey the Good Shepherd takes for his sheep.

PAUSE

In what do you invest your life? For what or whom would you lay down your life? Christ laid down his life for you – what, then, is your value?

PRAY ...*Thy kingdom come*

Invest a little time in silence and solitude today and let God speak to you about your true worth. Pray for those who look to you to shepherd them.

WITNESS ...*Thy will be done*

Make time today to care for someone, friend or stranger, with tenderness and goodness. Invest your love and time in them.

Wednesday, Week 5

Known

READ John 10.22-30

'My sheep hear my voice. I know them, and they follow me.'

The good shepherd protects and provides. The good shepherd invests his own life in the sheep. The good shepherd knows the sheep, and is known by them.

In the end, that is our deepest need and greatest joy: to know and, even more, to be known.

It's what we all search for. It's a gift we can give each other. It's the gift of God in Christ. To know and to be known, by love and in love, eternally.

We know Christ as we follow Christ. As we follow Christ we know Christ. It's gift and it's calling. It's a journey which leads us, with Christ, through death to life.

PAUSE

Who knows you well? What does it mean for you to be known, accepted and loved? What enables you to let yourself be seen, and known, and loved?

PRAY ...*Thy kingdom come*

Find a place today where you can be still and silent ... and realise that God knows and loves you. Then pray the same for others.

WITNESS ...*Thy will be done*

Refuse shallow judgements or labels, and get to know someone today, there's no short cut to sharing God's love.

Thursday, Week 5

I am the resurrection

READ John 11.17-27

Jesus said to her, 'I am the resurrection and the life. Those who believe in me, even though they die, will live.'

Jesus hears that his friend Lazarus is seriously ill. Strangely he doesn't rush to be with Lazarus and his sisters Martha and Mary, though they are close and deeply loved friends.

When he finally arrives, Lazarus is dead and has been buried for four days.

In her grief, and confusion about Jesus' absence, Martha expresses a tentative faith in God and a hope in life after death.

Jesus invites her to take a step of personal trust in him. 'I am the resurrection and the life... Do you believe this?' he asks. 'Yes, Lord, I believe,' she replies.

PAUSE

Think about your faith. What tests it? What strengthens it? How does your faith deepen and grow into a personal trust in Christ?

PRAY ...*Thy kingdom come*

Be still, be silent and, as you are able, pray with Martha: 'Yes, Lord, I believe.' Pray for all who in grief today reach out to God in faith and hope.

WITNESS ...*Thy will be done*

Make time today for resurrection — a word, a bunch of flowers, a prayer, a visit. Offer comfort in sadness and point to Christ the source of all hope and life.

Friday, Week 5

Grief

READ John 11.28-37

When Mary came where Jesus was and saw him, she knelt at his feet and said to him, 'Lord, if you had been here, my brother would not have died.'

Mary expresses her sorrow in the same words as her sister: 'if you had been here, Lord... '. She is heartbroken and cannot understand why Jesus did not come earlier.

She weeps. Jesus is 'deeply moved' and 'greatly distressed'. Jesus weeps.

Jesus has no words for Mary. There is no invitation to trust as there was for Martha. Simply Jesus' own tears from his broken heart.

His tears and pain take him to the grave of Lazarus, and deeply moved by his own grief and that of those around him Jesus cries out. He calls Lazarus out of the tomb.

PAUSE

Take time today to reflect on times of disappointment or bereavement you have been through? Where was God in these? How did he make his presence known?

PRAY ...*Thy kingdom come*

Pray for people who are broken-hearted and disappointed, for those who are at a loss or without hope. Pray for resurrection.

WITNESS ...*Thy will be done*

Make time today to notice the sadness of another, and be moved by it. Let that grief you feel enable you to cry out to God for them.

Saturday, Week 5

Trust

READ John 11.38-44

Jesus said to her, 'Did I not tell you that if you believed, you would see the glory of God?'

The stone is rolled away. Lazarus is summoned back to life. It's a sign of glory.

The glory of God that transforms our ordinariness and our pain, the glory of God that raises the dead to life.

Jesus the resurrection invites us to come to him and to put our trust in him. If you believe you will see the glory of God, in others and in yourself.

Jesus calls us, like Lazarus, out of the tombs that confine us and summons us to life. Be alive, he says. Live with joy as signs of God's glory.

PAUSE

What has challenged you in this week's reflections? How would you describe the life to which Jesus is inviting and calling you?

PRAY ...*Thy kingdom come*

Listen for the voice of Jesus, and, as you are able, respond. Pray for all who struggle to believe.

WITNESS ...*Thy will be done*

Seek the words and the opportunity to invite someone to trust in Jesus and, as they do so, to discover God's glory in their life.

Week 6
LEAVING

'Those who love their life lose it, and those who hate their life in this world will keep it for eternal life. Whoever serves me must follow me, and where I am, there will my servant be also.'
JOHN 12.25-26

Jesus prepares to leave. He is anointed at Bethany with love and fragrance. He is welcomed into Jerusalem with joy and song. Some people ask to see him and he shows them a seed falling to the ground.

My leaving, he says, is a death that will give life. I lay my life down that others, many many others, can live.

He invites us to follow him and make our own letting go. Our leaving of status so that we can, like him, kneel and wash feet. Our leaving of fear so that we can, in obedience to him, love one another.

I'm leaving, says Jesus, Will you follow me?

What might God be inviting you to let go of or leave behind? How might this enable you to follow Jesus' example of love and service and in so doing discover life?

**Fifth Sunday of Lent,
Week 6 (Passiontide begins)**

Perfume

READ John 12.1-8

Mary took a pound of costly perfume made of pure nard, anointed Jesus' feet, and wiped them with her hair. The house was filled with the fragrance of the perfume.

Passiontide begins today. It's the latter part of Lent when reflections turn to Jesus' journey to Jerusalem and his suffering – his passion – there. The journey begins in Bethany where Jesus returns to the home of Martha and Mary, and their brother Lazarus.

Mary, in an act of deep devotion – costly, fragrant and intimate – anoints Jesus' feet with perfume, wiping them with her hair.

Judas complains that this is wasteful extravagance. Could not the perfume have been sold and the money used to feed the poor?

Mary's loving act anoints the feet that will walk the painful path to the cross, and in doing so helps prepare and support Jesus for his own supremely costly act of love.

PAUSE
Reflect today on love and how we express it. In what ways is God's love made known to you? How does it touch you?

PRAY ...*Thy kingdom come*
Express your love for God; as you are able, use your body—kneeling, lifting hands, or in stillness.

WITNESS ...*Thy will be done*
Make time today for fragrance: a gift of perfume, burn some incense, touch someone's life with tenderness and love.

Monday, Week 6

Song

READ John 12.12-18

So they took branches of palm trees and went out to meet him, shouting, 'Hosanna! Blessed is the one who comes in the name of the Lord'

Jesus says goodbye to Bethany and walks the short distance to the Mount of Olives and from there down the hill into the city of Jerusalem.

He leaves the intimacy of the home of his friends and finds a noisy, joyful crowd waiting to welcome him. Loud, colourful, vibrant—a striking contrast to Mary's quiet moment of anointing. But, for these people also, this is an expression of love and readiness to follow.

Their song is one of praise, and it is also one of expectation and hope. It anticipates change. Blessed is the one who comes to lead us into a new future, for here is one who has brought someone back to life. He comes in humility, riding a donkey, not a stallion.

PAUSE

What might it mean for you to welcome Christ to share this day with you? What new future will he bring, and how does he bring it?

PRAY ...*Thy kingdom come*

With open hand and open heart, welcome Christ: 'Hosanna! Blessed is the one who comes in the name of the Lord.'

WITNESS ...*Thy will be done*

Offer a gift of hospitality today. Make space for someone in your home, in your diary, in your heart.

Tuesday, Week 6

A seed

READ John 12.20-26

'Very truly, I tell you, unless a grain of wheat falls into the earth and dies, it remains just a single grain; but if it dies, it bears much fruit.'

Lovingly anointed in Bethany; joyfully welcomed in Jerusalem; Jesus continues on his journey, his leaving. Some people make a request to his disciples: 'we wish to see Jesus'. Jesus' unexpected reply is to invite them to see God's glory, made visible in his suffering and death.

A seed falling, dying, lets go of life – it's a kind of leaving. Yet from that comes life. Not one solitary life reborn but abundant life, a plant giving birth to a whole harvest of fruit, with countless more seeds.

God's glory is seen in the life of Jesus. It is also seen in the death of Jesus and the abundance of life that comes from that. Jesus invites us to see that God's glory is similarly made visible in our own letting go.

PAUSE
Look for the signs of life around you, and reflect on the seeds which have produced it. Let God speak to you about your own life.

PRAY ...*Thy kingdom come*
Thank God for the willingness of Christ to let his life fall to the ground, and for the life that is yours through that. Pray for all who ask: 'we wish to see Jesus'.

WITNESS ...*Thy will be done*
Plant a seed today – in your garden, in a relationship or amongst the pains of the world.

Wednesday, Week 6

A light

READ John 12.27-36

Jesus said to them, 'The light is with you for a little longer. Walk while you have the light, so that the darkness may not overtake you. If you walk in the darkness, you do not know where you are going.

The shadows lengthen. The day is coming to an end. Jesus, the light, walks into the gathering darkness, taking leave of friends and followers, taking his leave of life.

The light seems fragile and vulnerable; the darkness, powerful and inescapable. His soul, he says is troubled. Should he ask God for a way out?

The light of trust still shines in Jesus. The light is bright enough to see the path ahead and strong enough for the love and courage to walk it.

Jesus invites us, when darkness is encroaching or persistent, to look for his light and follow it.

PAUSE

What feels as if it is darkness around you, or perhaps within you? What enables you to see the light that is Christ?

PRAY ...*Thy kingdom come*

Pray for those who 'walk in darkness' today – in fear or in grief, trapped or blinded. Pray that they, with you, will see the light of Christ.

WITNESS ...*Thy will be done*

Make time today to bring light into a situation. Choose truth. Seek justice. Walk in love alongside someone.

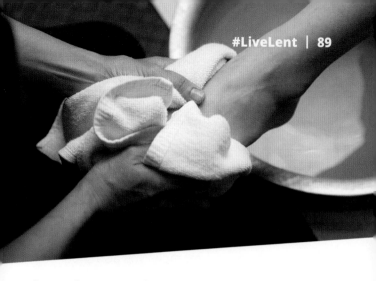

Thursday, Week 6

A servant

READ John 13.1-15

He got up from the table, took off his outer robe, and tied a towel around himself. Then he poured water into a basin and began to wash the disciples' feet.

As Jesus nears the end of his leaving, he shares one last meal with his disciples. It has been a journey of love and concludes in a meal of love, as John says, 'he loved them to the end'.

At the meal, as a leaving gift, he gives his disciples a sign. Just as Mary had lovingly anointed his feet, so he kneels before his friends and washes their tired and dusty feet.

He ties a towel around his waist, pours water into a bowl, and washes and wipes their feet. It is a physical act, a touch of love. This is his gift to them. The invisible God made visible. Glory seen and touched.

He offers it also as an example: 'you also should do as I have done to you'.

PAUSE
Reflect on Jesus' action. Imagine him washing your feet. What is it that he is doing for you and giving to you? How can you follow his example?

PRAY ...*Thy kingdom come*
Thank God for the love that kneels down and washes you. Pray for the humility to receive that gift and the grace to follow that example.

WITNESS ...*Thy will be done*
Make time today to serve someone else – practically, lovingly, unconditionally. Pray that they might glimpse God's glory and love.

Friday, Week 6

A command

READ John 13.31-35

I give you a new commandment, that you love one another. Just as I have loved you, you also should love one another.

A falling seed, a light challenging the dark, a kneeling servant... images of Jesus as he takes his leave and journeys into suffering and death.

What is it that shapes that journey? What leads him on? It is love. Simply love and supremely love. So Jesus offers his friends a second gift, a simple and supreme command: 'Love one another, as I have loved you.'

Love must shape our journey too. It is then that the glory of God is seen and others will know Christ in us.

PAUSE

Ask yourself what Jesus' command to his friends means in your life. Who are the ones you are called to love—as Christ loves you?

PRAY ...*Thy kingdom come*

Pray for the Church, the community of Jesus' disciples. Pray that we might hear afresh Jesus' command to love one another.

WITNESS ...*Thy will be done*

Make time today to restore a relationship that has been broken. Love one another.

Saturday, Week 6

A question

READ John 13.36-38

Jesus answered, 'Will you lay down your life for me? Very truly, I tell you, before the cock crows, you will have denied me three times.'

'Lord, where are you going?' asks Peter. I'm leaving, says Jesus.

Peter replies, I'll come with you, I'm ready to die for you.

Are you really ready to come with me? One day you will be. One day you will lay down your life for me. But not tonight.

Tonight Peter will fail Jesus. He will deny he even knows Jesus.

PAUSE

Ask yourself today what it is that Jesus calls you to be and do? Are there things that challenge you? Are there things that you are not ready for – yet?

PRAY ...*Thy kingdom come*

Pray for all who feel they have let Christ down, and for yourself in the things you get wrong... and right.

WITNESS ...*Thy will be done*

Make time today for failure and failures. Be gentle with yourself and with others.

Week 7
JOURNEY

Philip said to him, 'Lord, show us the Father, and we will be satisfied.' Jesus said to him, 'Have I been with you all this time, Philip, and you still do not know me? Whoever has seen me has seen the Father...' **JOHN 14.8-9**

At the beginning of his Gospel, John says 'No one has ever seen God. It is God the only Son, who is close to the Father's heart, who has made him known.' It is true of the baby in Bethlehem. It is true of the man of Galilee preaching and healing, calling and confronting. It is true of Jesus as he enters Jerusalem and journeys through his last week to his death on the cross.

As we see Jesus share a meal with his anxious disciples and give them peace, we see the Father.

As we see Jesus arrested, beaten, mocked and facing the injustice of fearful power, we see the Father.

As we see Jesus nailed to the cross, speaking words of forgiveness and love, we see the Father.

How might you, in your own context and in the strength that God gives, enable others to see the Father?

Palm Sunday, Week 7

I am the way

READ John 14.1-9

'I am the way, and the truth, and the life. No one comes to the Father except through me.'

Holy Week begins today as we celebrate Jesus' entry into Jerusalem: crowds cheering, branches waving. Today also marks the start of the last week of Jesus' life on earth, his journey to the cross and to death, and through death... to life.

Jesus says, I am the way. Walk with me, follow me, come with me to the Father.

To follow Jesus is not primarily to follow a code of practice or even a rule of life; it is to walk with him. At the beginning of his ministry he invited people to come and see, and live. At the end of his life he does the same. Let us journey with him.

PAUSE

Ask yourself what it will mean for you to walk, this week, with Jesus. Where might he take you? What might he show you?

PRAY ...*Thy kingdom come*

Ask God to open your eyes to see Jesus afresh and, as you do so, to see the way he opens for you. Pray for all who seek to walk with Jesus this week.

WITNESS ...*Thy will be done*

Make time today to walk with a friend, or to welcome a stranger. Speak to them of the one who is the way.

Monday of Holy Week, Week 7

I am the vine

READ John 15.1-11

I am the vine, you are the branches. Those who abide in me and I in them bear much fruit, because apart from me you can do nothing.

Jesus continues his conversation with his friends. He is leaving, his journey has begun. He is going to the Father, to prepare a place for them.

Yet, in his words and in the presence of the Spirit, he remains with them, and Jesus invites his friends to remain in him.

Jesus is not leaving them alone, but leading them into a new relationship and belonging. It is as deeply nurturing as the branches of a vine: it is life-giving and fruitful.

We journey, we live lightly in this world, but we are not cut off from each other or God.

PAUSE

Take time today to look at a tree. See the blossom or the buds, the leaves, the branches, the trunk and the roots. Let God speak to you about what it means to 'abide' in Jesus.

PRAY ...*Thy kingdom come*

Pray for all who today feel themselves cut off from the love or life of God, for all who feel they have to live life in isolation.

WITNESS ...*Thy will be done*

Reach out to someone who is on their own. Speak to them of the one who is love and belonging.

Tuesday of Holy Week, Week 7

Peace

READ John 16.25-33

*'I have said this to you, so that in me you may
have peace. In the world you face persecution.
But take courage; I have conquered the world!'*

What is it that will mark the life of Jesus'
friends? As they seek to walk with him, the
way, and live in relationship with him, the
vine, there is a new gift to be treasured.

‘My peace I give to you.’

Jesus journeys into the darkness of Gethsemane, the violence and cowardice of arrest and trial, and the horror of the cross. He does so with courage and in peace, not because he doesn’t realise what’s going on, but because he entrusts himself to God.

That same gift of peace is ours through him.

PAUSE
Reflect today on the pain of the world and struggles in your own life. Where in it all do you know God’s peace and the courage that comes through that peace?

PRAY ...*Thy kingdom come*
Receive the peace that is Christ’s gift to you. Pray for those walking through darkness today.

WITNESS ...*Thy will be done*
Make the effort to face something or someone you find difficult. Do so with courage and with peace and seek to bring God’s love.

Wednesday of Holy Week, Week 7

Arrest

READ John 18.1-27

Then Jesus, knowing all that was to happen to him, came forward and asked them, 'For whom are you looking?' They answered, 'Jesus of Nazareth.' Jesus replied, 'I am he.'

Soldiers seek out Jesus at night. His peace and courage are evident in the simplicity and gentleness of his words.

'I am he.'

Jesus knows why they have come. He knows also who he is. He speaks not with fearful resignation but with strength and quietness.

They are angry, anxious and armed, unsure of who he is or what they are really doing. The drama of this night begins to unfold.

PAUSE
Take time today to read the story of Jesus' arrest and let God speak to you through it.

PRAY ...*Thy kingdom come*
Pray that in your journey, in the things that are going on in your life at this moment, you will know who you are; and, in that, find peace and a quiet strength.

WITNESS ...*Thy will be done*
How might you 'come forward' and be available for those who look for you, or look to you, today?

Maundy Thursday, Week 7

Trial

READ John 18.28-40

So Pilate went out to them and said, 'What accusation do you bring against this man?'

Maundy Thursday gets its name from the Latin word *mandare* meaning to command. We remember Jesus' command to 'love one another' and his example of service in washing the feet of his friends.

In his birth, in his life and in this final week what we see in Jesus is love lived out, love in humanity, love in reality.

It is this love, the love of God made visible, which is on trial before religious and political leaders. There is, in the end, no real accusation; just blindness, angry defensiveness and fearful expediency.

If you stop and think about it, whether in our own hearts or in the world, it is just these things that continue to resist the power of God's love.

PAUSE
Take time today to read the story of Jesus' trial and let God speak to you through it.

PRAY *...Thy kingdom come*
Thank God for the love that faces up to fear, anger and blindness. Let that love stand tall and strong in your heart.

WITNESS *...Thy will be done*
Take a stand today. Quietly, peacefully, stand strong in the face of fear, dishonesty or prejudice.

Good Friday, Week 7
Death

READ John 19.1-30

When Jesus had received the wine, he said, 'It is finished.' Then he bowed his head and gave up his spirit.

Jesus' journey on earth moves to its completion. It ends, as it has always been lived, in trust.

Life received. Life lived. Life returned.

The wonder is that in the moment of letting go, that final act of trust, there is not defeat but victory. For in Jesus' offering of himself, in his final act of love, in his refusal to hate or meet violence with curse, in his offer of forgiveness, there is the promise of life and love for all.

Come, see, receive.

PAUSE
Take time today to read the story of Jesus' death and let God speak to you through it.

PRAY ...*Thy kingdom come*
In quietness, in thanks and in trust, offer your life to God afresh and pray for all who today are nearing the end of their lives.

WITNESS ...*Thy will be done*
Take an opportunity, on a walk of witness or in a quiet word, to speak of what it is that makes this Friday special and good.

Saturday in Holy Week, Week 7
Silence

READ John 19.31-42

Joseph of Arimathea, who was a disciple of Jesus, though a secret one, asked Pilate to let him take away the body of Jesus.

Jesus has died. His side and his heart pierced by a sword. His body and his love stretched to breaking point.

Most of Jesus' disciples – not least the men – have fled.

Like Nicodemus, Joseph of Arimathea has been a secret follower of Jesus. At this moment, when others have deserted Jesus, he comes forward and takes Jesus' body to be buried.

Jesus' wounded body is wrapped in cloth and perfume, and laid down to rest in love. It is an act of worship, silent and sad.

PAUSE

Take time today to be silent and still, and wait with Jesus. How might you, today, express your worship and your love?

PRAY ...*Thy kingdom come*

Pray for all who, for whatever reasons, are secret followers of Jesus.

WITNESS ...*Thy will be done*

Make time today to do something, silent and unseen, for someone else.

Easter Day

Encounter

READ John 20

Supposing him to be the gardener, she said to him, 'Sir, if you have carried him away, tell me where you have laid him, and I will take him away.' Jesus said to her, 'Mary!'

Mary Magdalene rises early to visit Jesus' tomb and finds the stone has been rolled away. She runs to tell Peter and John. They discover that the tomb is empty. But then they go home, leaving Mary alone.

Through the near darkness – and her tears – she notices someone. She thinks it must be the gardener. She hears Jesus speak her name. In that moment, in that voice and that person, Mary knows that love and life has come again.

She knows that the journey continues for her, and for all. Come, see, receive, live… and tell others.

The light shines. The darkness has not overcome it. Alleluia!

The light shines. Let your light shine. Alleluia!

PAUSE
Take time today to know that Christ is risen, that life and love has come again for you. Make some time in the coming week to note down some of what you have discovered of that life in these last six weeks.

PRAY *…Thy kingdom come*
Alleluia! Christ is risen! He is risen indeed! Alleluia!

WITNESS *…Thy will be done*
Make time today, like Mary, to go to your friends and tell them, 'I have seen the Lord.'

NEXT STEPS

Take part in Thy Kingdom Come

 *Thy Kingdom Come* is a global prayer movement that invites Christians around the world to pray for more people to come to know Jesus. What started in 2016 as an invitation from the Archbishops of Canterbury and York to the Church of England has grown into an international and ecumenical call to prayer.

During the 11 days of *Thy Kingdom Come* – between Ascension and Pentecost – it is hoped that everyone who participates will deepen their friendship with Jesus, bring other to know Jesus or know him better, and come to know that every aspect of their life is the stuff of prayer.

In 2018, *Thy Kingdom Come* takes place from 10th to 20th May. For more details and a wide range of resources visit www.thykingdomcome.global

Sign up for further discipleship campaigns

Visit www.churchofengland.org/lent or text LENT to 88802 to sign up by e-mail or text to take part in future discipleship initiatives for Easter 2017 and beyond from the Church of England. It is free to sign up and you can easily opt out at any time.

Published 2018 by Church House Publishing
www.chpublishing.co.uk
Church House, Great Smith Street, London SW1P 3AZ
© The Archbishops' Council 2018

Single ISBN 978 1 78140 082 1
Pk 10 ISBN 978 1 78140 083 8
Pk 50 ISBN 978 1 78140 084 5

Written by John Kiddle

The opinions expressed in this book are those of the author.

A catalogue record for this publication is available from the British
Library.

Design by www.penguinboy.net
Printed in the UK by Core Publications Ltd

Acknowledgements

Renewal & Reform

The **#LiveLent project** is part of the Church of England's **Renewal and
Reform programme**, aimed at helping us become a growing Church for
all people and for all places.

#Live Lent: Let Your Light Shine has been developed by The Ven. John
Kiddle in association with Thy Kingdom Come.

Church House Publishing would like to express warmest thanks to the
Diocese of Birmingham and to all involved in the original **Love Life Live
Lent project** and in helping to make it available nationwide since 2007.
We are also very grateful to the **Diocese of St Albans**, for whom John
Kiddle wrote the **Life Signs Lent challenge** on which Let **Your Light
Shine** is partly based.

Bible readings are taken from The New Revised Standard Version
(Anglicized Edition), copyright 1989, 1995 by the Division of Christian
Education of the National Council of the Churches of Christ in the United
States of America. All rights reserved.

Picture on p. 83 © Graham Lacdao, St Paul's Cathedral.